PRO WRESTLING LEGENDS

Steve Austin
The Story of the Wrestler They Call "Stone Cold"

Ric Flair
The Story of the Wrestler They Call "The Nature Boy"

Bill Goldberg

Bret Hart
The Story of the Wrestler They Call "The Hitman"

The Story of the Wrestler They Call "Hollywood" Hulk Hogan

Kevin Nash

Dallas Page
The Story of the Wrestler They Call "Diamond" Dallas Page

Pro Wrestling's Greatest Tag Teams

Pro Wrestling's Greatest Wars

Pro Wrestling's Most Punishing Finishing Moves

The Story of the Wrestler They Call "The Rock"

Randy Savage
The Story of the Wrestler They Call "Macho Man"

The Story of the Wrestler They Call "Sting"

The Story of the Wrestler They Call "The Undertaker"

Jesse Ventura
The Story of the Wrestler They Call "The Body"

The Women of Pro Wrestling

CHELSEA HOUSE PUBLISHERS

Ric Flair
The Story of the Wrestler
They Call "The Nature Boy"

Matt Hunter

Chelsea House Publishers
Philadelphia

Produced by Choptank Syndicate, Inc.

Editor and Picture Researcher: Mary Hull
Design and Production: Lisa Hochstein

CHELSEA HOUSE PUBLISHERS

Editor in Chief: Stephen Reginald
Production Manager: Pamela Loos
Art Director: Sara Davis
Director of Photography: Judy L. Hasday
Managing Editor: James D. Gallagher
Senior Production Editor: J. Christopher Higgins
Project Editor: Anne Hill
Cover Illustrator: Keith Trego

Cover Photos: Jeff Eisenberg Sports Photography

The Chelsea House World Wide Web site
address is http://www.chelseahouse.com

First Printing

1 3 5 7 9 8 6 4 2

Library of Congress Cataloging-in-Publication Data

Hunter, Matt
        Ric Flair: the story of the wrestler they call "The Nature Boy" / by Matt Hunter
            p. cm.— (Pro wrestling legends)
        Includes bibliographical references and index.
        Summary: A biography of the wrestler Ric Flair, known as the "Nature Boy."
        ISBN 0-7910-5825-5 — ISBN 0-7910-5826-3 (pbk.)
        1. Flair, Ric, 1949– —Juvenile literature. [1. Flair, Ric, 1949– . 2. Wrestlers.]
    I. Title. II. Series.

GV1196.F59 H56 2000
796.812'092—dc21
[B]
                                                              00-021865

Contents

THE LEGEND
MAY NEVER END

In 1998, after 26 years as a professional wrestler, Ric Flair was in trouble. His very career was in jeopardy. Ironically, the opponent who threatened to finish him once and for all stared at him from across a conference room table, not a professional wrestling ring.

"Nature Boy" Ric Flair had many legendary moments in his storied career, but there had also been many times when fans and fellow wrestlers counted him down-and-out. Each time, however, Flair managed to bounce back and prove the critics wrong.

Many thought Flair's streak had finally ended, though, in the spring of 1998, when Flair had an out-of-the-ring clash with then-president of World Championship Wrestling (WCW) Eric Bischoff. WCW's executive committee had granted Flair a leave of absence to attend a youth wrestling tournament to cheer on his son, Reid. When Bischoff found out what the committee had done, he became outraged and demanded that Flair cancel his plans and wrestle.

For many people, it would have been a difficult decision. On the one hand, there was an important family commitment. On the other hand, the boss had demanded that he show up for work no matter what the circumstances. In the world of

Angry because Hogan hadn't earned the WCW title Kevin Nash handed him in 1999, Flair went after the Hulkster. It was a tough battle, but Flair came away with his sixth WCW World title.

professional wrestling, long hours and many days and nights on the road are the norm. Wrestlers are expected to tour and their busy schedules do not always allow a lot of time for their families and friends. For Flair, choosing between work and family was an easy decision. WCWs executive committee had granted him the time he had asked for, and he was not about to miss his son's wrestling tournament. Outraged that Flair had ignored his order, Bischoff suspended him from WCW, and the battle spilled from the board room to the court-room as Bischoff called in his lawyers to try to pin the Nature Boy in a battle of legal muscle, claiming breach of contract. Flair called in his own legal team and mounted a powerful defense, but there were serious concerns as to whether he would be able to win.

As usual, the fans were the ones who suf-fered the most during this feud, as they were deprived of seeing the 15-time world champion in action until September 14, 1998, when the Nature Boy received a hero's welcome as he appeared before the fans in Greenville, South Carolina, during a live broadcast of the WCW *Monday Nitro* television program. Choking back emotions, Flair thanked fans for their over-whelming support and said that while legal problems remained, he was back for good. Better yet, he was going to be reforming the leg-endary Four Horsemen, the quartet of wrestlers that rose to National Wrestling Alliance (NWA) prominence in the mid-1980s.

The ovation was deafening, and the fans were thrilled, as were Arn Anderson, Dean Malenko, Chris Benoit, and Steve McMichael, who stood alongside Flair to form the new edition of the

Horsemen. If Flair was choking on emotion, however, Bischoff was sputtering with anger. He demanded that Flair's microphone be cut off.

In truth, Bischoff was scared. Flair's return to WCW and the reformation of the Four Horsemen posed a serious threat to the New World Order (NWO), the renegade group of wrestlers who had gained significant power in the federation, and with whom Bischoff had developed strong ties.

Over the next several months, the animosity between Bischoff and Flair grew stronger. Both men used their interview time to insult each other. As the weeks passed, the tension between the two men grew more intense. Finally, the inevitable match was signed between Flair and Bischoff, to take place on December 27, 1998, at the Starrcade pay-per-view event at the MCI Center in Washington, D.C.

The notion of Bischoff wrestling against Flair wasn't absurd. Though Flair had years of ring experience on his side, was three inches taller and outweighed Bischoff by about 60 pounds, the younger Bischoff was a former professional kickboxer and knew how to defend himself better than the typical businessman.

The WCW World title was not on the line in Flair's 1998 match (that prize was up for grabs in a bout between Kevin Nash and world champion Bill Goldberg). In the past, Flair had won four of his world titles at Starrcade cards, but this time the 15-time world champion was wrestling a WCW executive. It seemed like quite a comedown for Flair. But as it turned out, the match against Bischoff was simply another step in one of the Nature Boy's most cleverly thought-out plans.

Bischoff scored a pinfall win over Flair at Starrcade, although to accomplish this he had to hit Flair with a pair of brass knuckles handed to him by Curt Hennig. The wrestling world, however, will better remember what happened the day after Starrcade. That was when Flair and Bischoff wrestled again, on a live broadcast of WCW's *Monday Nitro*. This time they wrestled with the stipulation that the winner would gain administrative control of WCW itself. Just in case, the Four Horsemen guarded the ring from outside interference.

A bleeding Ric Flair emerges from a cage match. Though many people think the blood drawn during pro wrestling matches is fake, more often than not it is real. Wrestlers try hard not to actually hurt one another, but injuries are sometimes unavoidable.

To the delight of the crowd, the Nature Boy pummeled Bischoff, then placed him in his signature finishing maneuver, the figure-four leglock. Bischoff submitted, but Flair wasn't satisfied. To make sure that there would be no controversy, he went on to pin Bischoff. Flair had wrestled his way to control over the federation.

Flair, however, was a wrestler, not an administrator. His victory over Bischoff wasn't so much part of a desire to rule the WCW board room as it was a significant part of his plan to infuriate the NWO faction led by "Hollywood" Hulk Hogan. Flair humiliated Bischoff by forcing him to set up the ring, sell souvenirs, and even clean arena bathrooms. While he probably took some satisfaction in seeing his enemy suffering, the only real satisfaction Flair knew was wearing a world title belt around his waist, which he intended to do as soon as possible.

At Starrcade, Hogan's close friend, Kevin Nash, had won a controversial victory over Bill Goldberg for the world title. A week later, on January 4, 1999, Nash and Hogan shocked the wrestling world. Nash was supposed to be defending the title against Hogan, but as the two men made their way into the ring, it became clear that no such title defense was about to happen. Hogan and Nash stood face-to-face. Hogan poked Nash in the chest with his index finger, and Nash comically fell back to the mat. The "Hulkster" covered him for the three-count, and the title changed hands. Hulk Hogan was once again WCW World champion, thanks to his NWO friend Nash, who had practically handed the championship to him on a silver platter.

Flair, meanwhile, was about to proceed to the next step of his plan, which was to restore prestige to the title by defeating Hogan for the WCW championship belt. The match was signed for the WCW Uncensored pay-per-view on March 14, 1999. In the weeks leading up to the bout, the Nature Boy displayed an intensity he hadn't shown in years. His ring style demonstrated rulebreaking tactics he hadn't utilized in a long time. When it finally came to match time, the intensity was turned up a notch. Flair went after Hogan with a vengeance, causing much of the crowd to actually cheer for the then-hated Hulkster, who was truly the underdog of this match. Flair didn't care. He continued his assault, bloodying the champion and pummeling his way to his 6th WCW World title and his 16th world title overall.

"I look back on the past year and just cringe sometimes," Flair said in a postmatch press conference. "So much time wasted out of the ring. I feel a great deal of satisfaction now. There were times when I thought I would never feel this way again."

The world now realized that after all these years, the Nature Boy was still "the man"— a reference to Flair's frequent boasts to his challengers that "to be the man, you've got to beat the man." The world realized, too, that in a sport that was changing with lightning speed, and that had embraced the brashness of youth, a veteran with a keen eye and a steady strategy had once again ascended to the top. At the end of the 20th century, professional wrestling seemed to change from week to week and there was a constant barrage of newcomers, so it was somewhat reassuring to fans when Ric

Flair managed to emerge as a champion again and again.

Perhaps most remarkable about Flair's WCW World championship victory was that it came shortly after his 50th birthday, 24 years after doctors had told him that he should never again set foot in a wrestling ring.

2

A PROMISING FUTURE, A STUNNING TRAGEDY

Richard Morgan Fliehr was born February 25, 1949, in Edina, Minnesota, a suburb of Minneapolis. Flair's father was a prominent Minnesota physician, and his mother was an author with a particular interest in theater.

Flair was fortunate to have such educated and well-off parents, but in later years he was often criticized by wrestling opponents who made fun of him, saying he had been born with a silver spoon in his mouth.

As a child, Flair was a solid student, a pro wrestling fan who idolized Buddy Rogers (he would later adopt Rogers's "Nature Boy" nickname), and an excellent athlete. In high school he played basketball, and he was a Minnesota state high school wrestling champion in 1967. At Wayland Academy, a private school, he was a standout football star and was twice named All-State lineman. It was no surprise, then, that Flair attended the University of Minnesota on a football scholarship, playing offensive guard.

After two years of college, however, Flair got restless. He dropped out of school and decided he wanted to become a professional wrestler. One of his college classmates was Greg Gagne, the son of legendary Minnesota amateur and professional wrestling superstar Verne Gagne, who ran a pro wrestling

While wrestling with the NWA in the early 1970s, Flair developed his signature hairstyle—wavy bleached blond hair.

As a child, Ric Flair's wrestling idol was Buddy "Nature Boy" Rogers, who sported flowing capes and had a cocky attitude. When he became a wrestler, Flair patterned himself after Rogers and adopted his "Nature Boy" nickname.

training camp. Flair secured a spot in Gagne's 1972 class, and soon made a name for himself as one of the most talented athletes the camp had ever seen.

Flair learned the basics of the sport under the tutelage of former professional wrestler Billy Robinson as well as Gagne himself, a nine-time American Wrestling Association (AWA) World champion who was universally acknowledged as one of the greatest technical wrestlers of all time.

Sporting close-cropped brown hair and a surly scowl, Flair made his professional wrestling debut in the AWA on December 10, 1972. He wrestled to a draw with "Scrap Iron" George Gadaski, and followed up his debut by wrestling mostly undistinguished matches in the now-defunct AWA, which, at that time, was owned by Verne Gagne.

In 1974 Flair joined Jim Crockett Promotions, a member of the then-powerful NWA. At the time, Crockett promoted matches in North Carolina and South Carolina, and was preparing to expand his base of operations. In Flair, Crockett saw a star, and before long, so did the fans.

Slimmed down from the 260 pounds he carried in the AWA, and now sporting wavy bleached-blond hair, Flair was an instant sensation in the mid-Atlantic region. Already he had begun to emulate his childhood wrestling idol, Buddy Rogers, who would have a huge influence on the development of Flair's own wrestling persona. Like Rogers, Flair started wearing flashy capes, and he developed a signature strut to the ring.

It did not take long for Flair to establish himself as a formidable tag team wrestler, joining forces with Mid-Atlantic star Rip Hawk. Flair's first taste of championship gold came on July 4, 1974, when he and Hawk captured the Mid-Atlantic heavyweight tag team title from Paul Jones and Bob Bruggers in Greensboro, North Carolina.

Before too long, Flair began to establish himself as a singles star as well. He captured his first solo belt when he pinned Paul Jones on June 3, 1975, and won the NWA television title. The reign lasted for only a week before Jones won the belt back from Flair, but Flair learned that he enjoyed the feel of a championship belt around his waist. It was a feeling he would grow used to in the years to come, and he didn't have to wait very long to know that feeling again.

On September 20, 1975, Flair defeated Wahoo McDaniel in Hampton, Virginia, to become the NWA Mid-Atlantic heavyweight champion. This title no longer exists, but in the mid-1970s it was one of the most respected

In 1979, one of Flair's biggest rivals was Ricky "the Dragon" Steamboat, whom he defeated for the NWA U.S. heavy-weight title.

championship titles in the sport, akin to the WCW U.S. heavyweight title or the World Wrestling Federation (WWF) Intercontinental title today. The fact that Flair was able to capture such a prestigious belt so early in his career was viewed as a significant achievement. The only title he could have captured that would have been more impressive would have been the NWA World heavyweight championship itself.

Flair's career was beginning to pick up steam. In less than three years, he had wrestled in two major organizations and captured three major titles. The fans soon realized that he had the makings of a great professional wrestler. National wrestling magazines took note of Flair, commenting on his prowess. Meanwhile, Flair was eating in fine restaurants, staying in good hotels, and flying in private planes. Life was good.

Then everything he had achieved came crashing down—literally. On October 4, 1975, Flair was flying to Wilmington, North Carolina, with several other wrestlers and officials of Jim Crockett Promotions in a Cessna 310 airplane. The plane crashed. Two occupants of the plane, Tim Woods and David Crockett, escaped from the accident with just cuts and scratches. Another one of the passengers, wrestler Johnny Valentine, broke his back and was paralyzed as a result of the accident. The pilot of the plane died from his injuries. Flair emerged from the plane's wreckage with a back that was broken in three different places, but he was lucky to be alive.

After receiving medical treatment, Flair received news from doctors that he did not

Flair teamed with Greg "the Hammer" Valentine, far right, in 1976 to win the Mid-Atlantic tag team title away from Gene and Ole Anderson.

want to hear. It was going to take at least a year for him to recover fully from the injuries he had sustained in the plane crash. Furthermore, his doctors advised him that he should never again set foot inside a wrestling ring. The injuries to his back had been severe, and the doctors warned him that an additional ring injury might cripple him for life.

Flair didn't like what the doctors told him. Determined to do something about it, he underwent extensive physical therapy. Flair worked very hard to heal his body and get himself back into good physical shape. Despite what the doctors had told him, he had no intention of giving up on his wrestling career.

Ultimately, he proved everyone wrong when he made a near-miraculous return to the ring on February 1, 1976, defeating his Mid-Atlantic heavyweight championship rival Wahoo McDaniel.

Had Flair gone out and wrestled the one match to prove he could do it, then spent a year to let his body heal, nobody would have thought any less of the Nature Boy. Flair, however, made a full-fledged comeback. The feud with McDaniel had been revisited in full force. On May 24, 1976, Flair and McDaniel met in a match in Charlotte, North Carolina, in which McDaniel put his Mid-Atlantic belt up against Flair's hair. If he lost the match, Flair would have to cut off the long, bleached-blond locks that had become a big part of his image as a wrestler. The Nature Boy emerged from the ring with his hair intact and his second Mid-Atlantic title reign underway.

Over the next few years, the Flair legend continued to grow along with his impressive list of championships. He finished 1976 with several more Mid-Atlantic title reigns, as he and McDaniel traded the belt back and forth. Ric also captured the Mid-Atlantic tag team title with Greg "the Hammer" Valentine, defeating Gene and Ole Anderson on Christmas day in Greensboro, North Carolina.

In 1977, Flair finally tasted World championship gold as he and Valentine captured the NWA World heavyweight tag team title. He also held the Mid-Atlantic tag team championship with Valentine, and captured solo titles by winning

Flair sports a purple sequined version of his trademark cape in the ring before an NWA match.

the NWA television title from Rufus R. "Freight Train" Jones, and the U.S. heavyweight championship from the legendary Bobo Brazil.

The momentum continued into 1978 as Flair's impact on the record books continued to grow. He won the U.S. heavyweight title from scientific legend Mr. Wrestling, and teamed with John Studd to capture the Mid-Atlantic tag team title from Paul Jones and Ricky "the Dragon" Steamboat.

The following year, Flair downed Steamboat on April 1 for the U.S. heavyweight title, and joined forces with Blackjack Mulligan to defeat Paul Jones and Baron Von Raschke on August 8 for his second NWA World tag team title.

As the '70s were drawing to a close, Flair faced a tough decision that would ultimately change the direction of his professional wrestling career. He was an excellent tag team wrestler, and had the championship record to prove it, but he was also a superb singles wrestler. He couldn't go on splitting his career between tag team and singles competition. He decided to focus his career primarily on singles wrestling.

His decision proved fateful. The 1980s—and wrestling immortality—were just around the corner for Flair.

3

THE FIRST OF MANY

Ric Flair had to wrestle with a problem before he could wrestle any opponents. To some fans, and in some ways to himself, the new Nature Boy was in the shadow of the original Nature Boy, Buddy Rogers.

Rogers had been popular in the 1960s. He held the NWA World championship from June 30, 1961, through January 24, 1963. More than the championships, though, Rogers was known for his blond hair, smirking expressions, and most of all, his legendary strut to the ring.

Though it was 1979, more than a decade and a half since Rogers last wore the NWA World heavyweight belt around his waist, "Nature Boy" Ric Flair wanted to exorcise the demons of the original Nature Boy and move on with his career. He decided to wrestle Rogers.

In a remarkable battle of Nature Boy vs. Nature Boy, Flair and Rogers stepped into the ring in Greensboro, North Carolina, on July 8, 1979. The atmosphere was electric, and the match came to an amazing finish when Flair defeated Rogers, using the figure-four leglock, Flair's signature move, but one that Rogers himself had popularized. In a rematch on July 16 in Spartanburg, South Carolina, Flair won again.

Ric "Nature Boy" Flair puts Kevin Von Erich in the sleeperhold. The Von Erich brothers, who were the most popular wrestlers in Texas, frequently challenged Flair.

on doing exactly what I'm doing right now. I intend to hold onto this championship for a very long time.

"The title means everything to me. If I have to wrestle more aggressively in order to hold onto the championship, I'm going to do just that. Once that belt is handed to you, you're not the same person. I knew it as soon as that gold buckle touched my hand. The thought ran through my mind that from this second on, since I am now the champion, my life will never be the same again."

His first title reign lasted nearly two years, until Harley Race ended it on June 10, 1983.

Flair knew one thing with absolute and complete certainty: he had to get the title back.

November 24, 1983, was a remarkable day in pro wrestling for many reasons. It was the day that Flair would begin his second NWA World title reign, regaining the belt from Race in Greensboro, North Carolina. It was also the occasion of the NWA's Starrcade '83 card.

Coming 16 months before the first WrestleMania, Starrcade was the original supercard. Those were the days before pay-per-view television, but Starrcade was a closed-circuit success, broadcast at dozens of locations in the United States as well as parts of the Caribbean. There were several memorable matches on the card. Roddy Piper pinned Greg Valentine in a bloody dog collar chain match to capture the U.S. title, and Rick Steamboat and Jay Youngblood regained the NWA World tag team championship from Jack and Jerry Brisco. Flair entered the ring a challenger and emerged a champion. More than a champion, though, he was the focal point of the biggest card of the year. Wrestling was growing in popularity. Closed-circuit television would soon give way to pay-per-view events. The sport was breaking out of its regional mindset and becoming national in scope. Ric Flair was right there at the center of it all.

The Nature Boy's second title reign lasted about four months, until Harley Race regained the belt in New Zealand. Flair followed Race from New Zealand to Singapore, where he clipped Race's reign short at just two days. Flair's third reign was underway.

When May 6, 1984, rolled around, Flair's title seemed to be in big trouble. His challenger at Texas Stadium in Irving, Texas, was Kerry Von Erich. At the time, the Von Erichs were by far the most popular wrestlers in Texas history and among the most popular wrestlers in the world. Kerry not only had the home ring advantage, he had the raw emotions of more than 43,000 fans on his side, since Kerry's brother, David, had died three months earlier while on a wrestling tour of Japan. Kerry was dedicating this title match to the memory of his brother. All of Texas—indeed, all of pro wrestling—seemed to be behind him.

Kerry won the NWA belt, but like Race before him, the reign didn't last long. Flair trailed Von Erich through Texas, and finally to Japan where, on May 24, he regained the belt in Yokosuka City.

Flair's nemesis, "American Dream" Dusty Rhodes, ended Flair's fourth title reign after two years and two months, but again, as he had done with Von Erich and Race, the Nature Boy came back with a vengeance, defeating Rhodes two weeks later. In fact, from the time he won his second NWA World title at Starrcade '83 until he lost his fifth NWA World title to Ronnie Garvin on September 25, 1987, Flair went a total of only 34 days in nearly four years without the NWA World championship belt around his waist.

Being the sport's top target, though, was beginning to affect Flair. "It's been like some sort of crazy battle royal or something," he told *Pro Wrestling Illustrated* magazine. "except that it's fifty against one. Fifty contenders against one champion. There's nothing like it anywhere else in sport, and it's a terrible amount of pressure to put on one man. If you're a contender, you can lose a match and there will always be tomorrow's match, or the next day. For me, I can't afford to let my concentration lapse for even a second. If I lose, that's it, the whole championship goes out the window. It's a matter of having everything I've geared my life to being put on the line each and every match. It's a do-or-die situation each time I step into the ring."

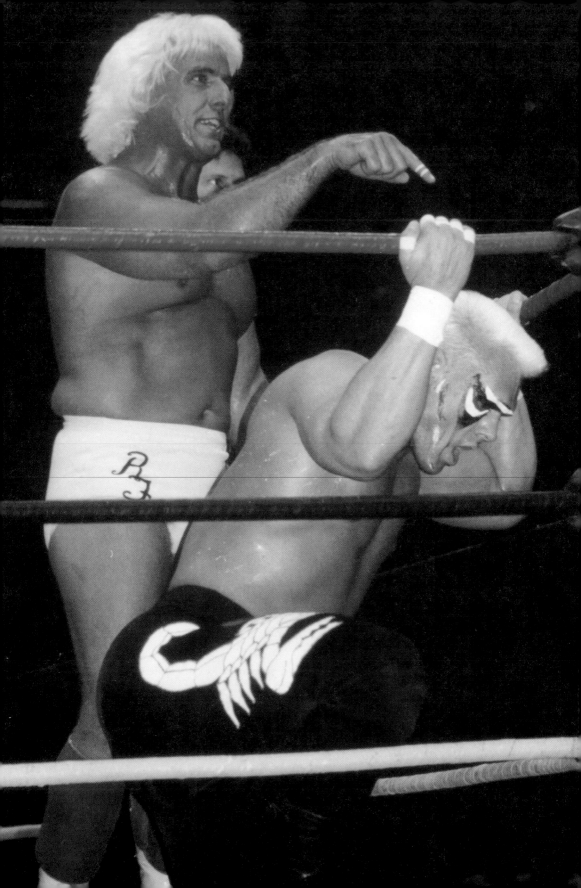

4 | THE FOUR HORSEMEN

Unlike the NWO, which sprang into being in mid-1996 with great drama and fanfare, the clique known as the Four Horsemen developed slowly and methodically a decade earlier. Ric Flair had always had his inner circle of close friends, relatives, and business associates. They all looked out for each other—and they especially looked out for Flair. As NWA World champion, Flair commanded power and prestige. He could lavish his praise on a wrestler and use his leverage as world champion to help make or break the careers of other wrestlers.

Among Flair's inner circle in mid-1986 were Tully Blanchard, a Texas-tough brawler who had held the U.S. heavyweight title for four months in 1985; Arn Anderson, a cousin to Flair and one of the all-time best tag team wrestlers, who won the NWA television title in January 1986 and wore the belt for eight months; Ole Anderson, another cousin to Flair and another excellent tag team grappler who had held the NWA World tag team title with his brother, Gene Anderson; and James J. Dillon, a smart manager and even smarter businessman who knew the ins and outs of both the wrestling ring and the corporate board room.

In 1990, Flair enjoyed a lengthy feud with his rival Sting, who had once been a member of the Four Horsemen.

In 1985, the careers of Blanchard, the Andersons, and Dillon became intertwined with that of Flair. Together, they seemed to be setting the pace of matters in the NWA.

In the summer of 1985, the de facto grouping of four wrestlers and one manager appeared on a broadcast of World Championship Wrestling on SuperStation TBS. Gloating about some damage they had caused to their opponents, Arn spoke: "The only time this much havoc has been wreaked by this few people, you need to go

Flair's cousin Arn Anderson, shown wrestling an opponent, coined the term "the Four Horsemen" for the clique of wrestlers loyal to Flair.

Ric Flair uses his signature figure-four leglock to subdue the Horsemen's rival, Magnum T.A.

all the way back to the Four Horsemen of the Apocalypse." The name stuck, and wrestling's most infamous collective was formalized.

Tops on the list of the Horsemen's enemies were Dusty Rhodes and Magnum T.A. On one memorable occasion, Rhodes and Magnum held Ole Anderson down on the mat while inviting their friend and protégé, Sam Houston, to try to break Anderson's leg.

The Horsemen's first great defining moment came on July 21, 1985. Blanchard was challenging Magnum T.A. for the U.S. heavyweight title in Charlotte, North Carolina. When Magnum executed a belly-to-belly suplex on Blanchard, Tully's leg hit the referee, knocking him out to such a degree that he was unable to score Magnum's pin on Blanchard. Suddenly, Blanchard's valet, Baby Doll, appeared out of the audience (she had been disguised as a security guard) and handed Blanchard a foreign object that he used on Magnum to score the pinfall and win the title.

The win was significant not only for the style in which it happened, but because once Tully strapped the U.S. title around his waist, all the Horsemen were wearing championship gold; Flair was NWA World heavyweight champion, and Ole and Arn wore the National tag team championship belts.

As the Horsemen grew in influence, it became clear that while having all the Horsemen wearing title belts was a goal for the group, it was not the only goal for the group. Their collective priority was to protect Flair and his World heavyweight championship. Indeed, 1986 was a very good championship year for Flair, who held the NWA World title for all but 14 days.

In early 1987, doubts began to be raised about Ole Anderson's loyalty to the group. In reality, Ole wanted to take some extra time off from the ring wars to spend a little more time with his son, but the familial excuse didn't sit well with his Horsemen brethren. On March 1, in a memorable interview aired on TBS, the Horsemen confronted Anderson, who hit Blanchard, cursed Dillon, and stormed off the set. The Four Horsemen were suddenly down by one Horseman. On March 14, Lex Luger became a full-fledged member of the Horsemen after a couple weeks as an associate Horseman. The association seemed to work very well, and the Horsemen seemed stronger than ever. In 1987, Flair remained world champion for all but two months and one day, and the organization also notched its first NWA World tag team title that year as Arn Anderson and Tully

Shortly after Flair won the NWA World title on February 20, 1989, former NWA World champion Terry Funk attacked him, using a brutal piledriver to break the vertebrae in Flair's neck. Even though wrestling matches are scripted and wrestlers do not intentionally try to injure one another, wrestlers sometimes sustain serious injuries in the ring.

Blanchard captured those belts from the Rock 'n' Roll Express on September 29. Meanwhile, Luger had taken the U.S. heavyweight title from Nikita Koloff on July 11.

As December rolled around, however, there were rumblings of discontent within the Horsemen. Luger had lost the U.S. title to Dusty Rhodes on November 26, the same day Flair had regained the world title from Ronnie Garvin. Perhaps perceiving a shift of power within the Horsemen back to Flair, and certainly fed up with being part of an organization for which he had to subsume his own individual career goals, Luger took his anger into the ring in Miami Beach, Florida, on December 2, 1987. The occasion was a Bunkhouse Stampede battle royal, the end of which found Dillon and Luger as the last two men in the ring. Dillon ordered Luger to throw himself over the top rope in order to let the Horsemen's manager win the bout. Luger refused, and won cheers from the fans when he threw Dillon over the top rope. Luger's association with the Horsemen had come to an end.

With Flair's blessing, many other wrestlers have been Horsemen over the years. Barry Windham joined the organization in 1988. Sting was made an official Horseman in 1990 (though his membership lasted only a month). Sid Vicious was a Horseman in 1990, and Woman became a Horsemen advisor. Later in the 1990s, the Horsemen roster included Curt Hennig, Steve McMichael, Brian Pillman, Chris Benoit, Jeff Jarrett, and Dean Malenko.

As 1988 progressed, the Horsemen met with a great deal of championship success. For a good portion of the year, all members of the group wore title belts: Flair was NWA World champion, Windham was U.S. heavyweight champion, and Blanchard and Anderson wore the NWA World tag team belts. It came as little surprise to anyone that James J. Dillon ended the year being voted Manager of the Year by the readers of *Pro Wrestling Illustrated* magazine. For the Horsemen, life was good, but for Flair, life was about to get worse.

The Nature Boy entered 1989 confident, but soon realized this year would not proceed as

smoothly as the last one. Flair was stunned by
Rick Steamboat, who captured the world title
on February 20, 1989. He regrouped to regain
the title on May 7, at the NWA's Wrestle War '89
pay-per-view card, but his celebration upon
winning the title was short-lived. Former NWA
World champion Terry Funk wanted a shot at
the belt, so he attacked Flair right after the
match. The piledriver that Funk used to send
Flair crashing through a wooden ringside table
cracked a vertebrae in Flair's neck and partially
ruptured a disc in his back. Flair was out of
action for 76 days.

When Flair returned, he had one thing on
his mind: revenge. The Funk-Flair wars characterized pro wrestling for most of the latter
half of the year and culminated November 15,
1989, at the nationally televised Clash of the
Champions IX card. Flair defeated Funk in the
main event, forcing Funk to shake his hand
and concede defeat. The feud, which also revi-
talized the Horsemen as an organization, was
voted Feud of The Year by the readers of *Pro
Wrestling Illustrated*, who also named Flair the
Wrestler of the Year for the fifth time. Readers
also chose Blanchard and Anderson Tag Team
of the Year and recognized the May 7, 1989,
Flair vs. Steamboat bout as Match of the Year.
For Flair, it was yet another remarkable year in
an incredible wrestling career that was growing
more amazing with time.

A feud with Sting was one of the corner-
stones of 1990 for Flair. The Nature Boy was
taken to a 45-minute draw by Sting at the
nationally televised Clash of the Champions I on
March 27, 1988 and ever since the two had
been rivals. Sting finally caught up with Flair

on July 7, 1990, in Baltimore, Maryland, bringing Flair's seventh NWA World title reign to a close.

Flair managed to win the title back from Sting on January 11, 1991. The Nature Boy's eighth NWA World title was, simultaneously, his first WCW World title. The sport was undergoing changes, and millionaire businessman Ted Turner had purchased Jim Crockett Promotions, the largest member of the NWA, in November 1988. Turner's SuperStation TBS broadcast World Championship Wrestling programs featuring NWA stars, and over the months that followed, the lines between the NWA and WCW were blurred. Ultimately, WCW withdrew from the NWA, but in 1991, Flair was acknowledged as the WCW/NWA World champion.

That year WCW issued a press release on July 2, with the headline, "Ric Flair and WCW To Part Company." It read:

> World Championship Wrestling (WCW) is saddened to report that after extensive negotiations with "Nature Boy" Ric Flair, stretching over the course of nearly one year, the parties have been unable to arrive at a mutually satisfactory contractual relationship. As a result, the WCW board has decided that the best course of action for WCW and its fans is to declare the World Championship title vacant and determine a new champion at the Great American Bash pay-per-view event in Baltimore, Sunday, July 14. Lex Luger, the number-one contender and current United States champion, will remain on the title card at the Bash. His opponent will be determined by the WCW board and announced at a date to be determined.

"I want to thank Ric Flair for all he has done for WCW in the past and wish him all the best for the future," said Jim Herd, executive vice president of WCW. "He has been a great champion."

Luger battled Barry Windham at the Bash and went on to win the WCW World title. Flair, meanwhile, was competing in a place where nobody who had watched the Nature Boy's career ever thought he would wind up. The NWA and WCW legend defected to a rival federation: the WWF.

THE NWA/WCW LEGEND DEFECTS

5

For years, Flair had appeared on interviews and talked about "walking that aisle," referring to the pathway between the dressing room area and the ring itself. He would say things like, "When I walk that aisle, the world will know what's causin' all this!" or "If you wanna be the man, you've got to beat the man, and I'm the man, so to beat me, you gotta have the guts to walk that aisle!" He had been walkin' that aisle in NWA and WCW rings for almost 20 years. The sight of the Nature Boy walking the aisle to a WWF ring was truly unthinkable, and nothing short of a shock to wrestling fans around the world.

The WWF in 1991 was the complete opposite of everything Flair had stood for throughout his entire wrestling career. The WWF was frequently referred to as a "circus," with Tito Santana transforming to El Matador, Rick Steamboat becoming "the Dragon," and Tony Atlas wrestling as Saba Simba. WWF franchise Hulk Hogan was appearing in terrible low-budget movies like *Suburban Commando*, and wrestlers with absurd personas like Berserker, Skinner, and Kato, littered the WWF landscape.

The Nature Boy made his entry into the WWF quietly. On September 10, 1991, he defeated Jim Powers in Cornwall,

When Flair defected to the WWF in 1991, fans couldn't wait for the first match between the Nature Boy and Hulk Hogan—a bout that Flair won.

Ontario, using his signature figure-four leglock to force Powers to submit. Flair's first match in the WWF was a success, although not a highly publicized one. The match wasn't aired on pay-per-view television, and his arrival wasn't trumpeted with brash announcements.

Word of Flair's arrival spread quickly, though, and many of his fans feared that the WWF would hand the Nature Boy a new persona, as they had done with so many other wrestlers who had joined the federation. But the WWF allowed Flair to be Flair, and the wrestling world breathed a collective sigh of relief. With so many wrestlers changing names and personas at the drop of a hat, it was nice to see someone stick to their character.

Meanwhile, the buzz began building for the inevitable matchup between Ric Flair and Hulk Hogan. Fans couldn't wait. After all, the speculation had gone on for years. Hogan was the star of the WWF, while Flair was an NWA legend. The first-ever match between Flair and WWF World champion Hogan took place on October 23, 1991, in Dayton, Ohio. Amazingly, it wasn't a pay-per-view card. It wasn't even a prime-time network television broadcast, but it was historic, and Flair won the match by countout.

As shocked as the fans were when Flair had defected to the WWF, they became puzzled by the way the WWF treated the NWA legend, keeping him out of the spotlight. Was the WWF forcing the Nature Boy to pay his dues, despite his 20 years as an NWA legend? Was this the WWF's way of proving that they were superior to the NWA? Was Flair being treated as a second-class wrestler out of spite and jealousy?

That certainly seemed to be the case at the November 27, 1991, Survivor Series, which was where Flair made his WWF pay-per-view debut. The Nature Boy didn't wrestle in the main event; that title match was reserved for The Undertaker, though Flair did interfere in that match. Instead, Flair was teamed with the Mountie, Ted DiBiase, and the Warlord in a Survivor Series match against "Rowdy" Roddy Piper, Bret "Hitman" Hart, Virgil, and "British Bulldog" Davey Boy Smith. Flair pinned Smith at the

No longer friends with Curt Hennig, Flair feuded with "Mr. Perfect," and lost a "loser leaves the WWF" match to Hennig in 1993.

10:55 mark, and his team won after 22:48 when the opposing team was disqualified.

It was a respectable showing for the Nature Boy, but Flair was still far from owning the spotlight the way he did in the NWA. His interference in the Undertaker-Hogan bout at the Survivor Series, though, helped shift the WWF spotlight. While involving himself in the title match, Flair had knocked WWF President Jack Tunney unconscious. The ensuing melee saw Undertaker's manager, Paul Bearer, also interfering by attempting to hit Hogan with an urn. Hogan ducked, and Bearer hit Undertaker instead. Hogan grabbed a fistful of ashes out of the urn, threw them in Undertaker's face, then pinned him.

The next day, in light of the chaos at the Survivor Series, Tunney declared the WWF World title vacant. He further declared that the new champion would be determined at the Royal Rumble, to be held January 19, 1992, in Albany, New York.

This was Flair's chance to shine, and he did. The Royal Rumble is a unique style of match involving 30 wrestlers. Two wrestlers start the match in the ring, and a new wrestler enters the ring every two minutes. The order of entry into the ring is very important and is determined by blind draw. The wrestler entering the ring later in the match has the greater advantage, because he is fresher and has fewer rivals to contend with.

Flair was the third man to enter the ring. When the night was over, though, he was the last to leave. Incredibly, Flair had outlasted all 29 WWF stars, and his time in the ring lasted an astonishing 62 minutes and two seconds.

The Nature Boy eliminated such formidable opponents as the British Bulldog, Big Bossman, and Randy Savage. Finally, he threw Sid Justice over the top rope at the 62:02 mark. Flair had captured his first WWF World title with an amazing show of strength and endurance.

Though Flair was famous for his longevity as a champion in the NWA and WCW, his luck was not as good in the WWF. Flair's second WWF pay-per-view appearance was at WrestleMania VIII on April 5, 1992, in Indianapolis, Indiana, where he lost the WWF World heavyweight championship title to Randy "Macho Man" Savage. While the loss must have been disappointing, Flair later counted the match among his most memorable career moments, right up there with his many NWA victories.

"It was a great thrill winning [the NWA World title] in Kansas City, Missouri, the first time," Flair recalled in a 1993 interview, "but when I won it back in Greensboro, North Carolina, in front of my home crowd, that was the biggest thrill for me until I got to WrestleMania. Walking out in Indianapolis in front of 70,000 folks was really big-time."

Though Flair's championship longevity didn't carry over to the WWF, his determination to regain a title certainly did. Flair regained the belt from the Macho Man at a WWF television taping on September 1, 1992, thanks to interference

Bret "Hitman" Hart was one of Flair's greatest opponents in the WWF.

from Razor Ramon. Flair lost the belt a month later, on October 12, to Bret Hart.

Meanwhile, Flair and his close friend, "Mr. Perfect" Curt Hennig, had been having problems. A tag team feud erupted, with Flair and Ramon battling Hennig and Savage. The Nature Boy's focus was split. On the one hand, he had a tag team feud to contend with, while on the other hand, he wanted to concentrate on regaining the world title from Hart. It was a dilemma he had encountered earlier in his career.

Flair and Hart wrestled in dozens of matches during the closing months of 1992 and the opening days of 1993, but the Nature Boy was unable to regain the title he so dearly wanted. Perhaps their most celebrated bout was the one Flair considered their best WWF match: a 60-minute marathon on January 9, 1993, in Boston.

On January 18, 1993, Flair's split focus between tag team and singles wrestling got the best of him, and the tag team feud in which he was involved led to a "loser leaves the WWF" bout with Curt Hennig. The Nature Boy lost the match. Yet Flair wrestled a few more WWF matches after losing to "Mr. Perfect," and his last bout in the WWF was a match against Bret Hart in Dortmund, Germany, on February 10, 1993.

Flair's WWF tenure ended not with a bang, but with a whimper. It was as if the Nature Boy had run out of steam. He found himself in the same situation he had been in back in 1979, when he made the crucial decision to focus exclusively on singles matches. As before, Flair was not benefiting from his split between singles and tag team competition and had to choose between the two. In that respect, his career had come full circle.

Ric Flair's career would come full circle in another respect, too: 11 days after wrestling his final WWF match, the Nature Boy returned to WCW. Once again, his decision was a fateful one.

6 BACK TO WCW

A t SuperBrawl III on February 21, 1993, Flair reappeared in WCW. Flair didn't wrestle that night, but his presence in Asheville, North Carolina, became the talk of the sport. What would the Nature Boy do next? Would he reform the Four Horsemen? Would he go after former Horseman partner Barry Windham for the NWA title, or target Big Van Vader for the WCW title?

Flair seemed to have targeted both titles. On June 17, 1993, he teamed with Arn Anderson to battle Brian Pillman and Steve Austin. At Flair's first pay-per-view appearance after returning to WCW, he pinned Barry Windham to capture the NWA title at Beach Blast '93 on July 18. That reign lasted until September 19, after which time he turned his attention to the massive and violent Vader, winning the WCW title at Starrcade on December 27. The match lasted 21:11, and signaled to the world that Flair's days as champion were far from over.

The Nature Boy dismissed Vader as a challenger once again when the two men wrestled at the SuperBrawl IV pay-per-view on February 20, 1994. Two months later, at Spring Stampede, Flair defeated his longtime rival, Rick Steamboat, in a battle that saw each man pin the other simultaneously.

When Flair left the WWF, his rival Hulk Hogan followed him, and the two resumed their war in WCW.

Flair won his ninth
NWA title by beating
Barry Windham,
bottom, on
July 18, 1993, at
Bash on the Beach.

WCW Commissioner Nick Bockwinkel ruled in Flair's favor, and the Nature Boy remained champion. A month later, Flair successfully defended his title against Windham at the Slamboree pay-per-view.

Then, as it had been when Flair left WCW to join the WWF, something unthinkable happened. WWF legend Hulk Hogan joined WCW. The Hulkster's first WCW appearance took place at Clash of the Champions XXVII on June 24, 1994, when Hogan saved WCW International champion Sting from a two-on-one attack by Flair and "Sensational" Sherri Martel. Later in the evening, Flair defeated Sting to unify the two titles, but he clearly had his eye on Hogan, and vice-versa.

"I'm in WCW because I've got some unfinished business with Flair," Hogan said, and indeed he had. If wrestling fans remained unsatisfied by the way the Hogan vs. Flair bouts went when Flair was in the WWF, so, too, did Hogan. He wanted to settle the score once and for all.

So when it came time for WCW's Bash at the Beach pay-per-view event, on July 17, 1994, Hogan was ready. It took him 21 minutes and 50 seconds to defeat the Nature Boy and capture the WCW World title.

The Flair-Hogan war consumed WCW. Immediately after Bash at the Beach, a Hogan-Flair rematch was signed for the nationally televised Clash of the Champions XXVIII card on August 24. Early in the card, Hogan was viciously attacked by a masked man, and it looked as if he would not be able to wrestle, but he staggered out of his hospital bed and made his way to the arena and the ring, where he lost to Flair by countout.

A loser-must-retire cage match between Hogan and Flair was signed for the October 23, 1994, Halloween Havoc pay-per-view card. Hogan pinned the Nature Boy to retain his WCW World title and end Flair's career—or so he thought.

Flair may not have been able to wrestle, but he was able to remain in WCW. He patched up his differences with Big Van Vader and man-aged the big man for his feud against the Hulkster in early 1995. Flair kept interfering in matches on behalf of Vader, and Hogan's frustration level grew so high that he asked the WCW executive committee to rescind the Halloween Havoc retirement stipulation. They did, and Flair returned to WCW as an active wrestler.

Meanwhile, the Nature Boy had scored yet another career high point. This one took place on April 29, 1995, in Pyongyang, North Korea. An estimated crowd of 190,000 was on hand at Mayday Stadium for a wrestling card that was part of the three-day Pyongyang International Sports and Culture Festival. The main event: Ric Flair vs. Japanese legend Antonio Inoki. It was the first-ever match between these two veteran superstars. Inoki got the better of Flair, defeating him in 14:52, before the biggest crowd ever assembled in pro wrestling history.

On December 27, 1995, Flair captured his third WCW World title by defeating Randy Savage in just eight minutes, 41 seconds at Starrcade. The resulting Flair-Savage feud was even more vicious and violent than it had been in the WWF, and the Macho Man regained the belt just a month later, in Las Vegas. The championship was back in Flair's hands a month later, when he defeated Savage on February 11, 1996.

Flair and Savage's feud dissipated when a new challenger appeared on the horizon: The Giant. The massive (7' 4" and 430 pound) rook-ie had only six months of pro experience under his belt, but he managed to unseat Flair for the WCW World title on April 22, 1995, during a live broadcast of WCW's *Monday Nitro* television program. The defeat seemed to take more than the usual toll on Flair. Usually, the Nature Boy would rebound from a loss and target the new champion with an intensity that won him back the title in a matter of weeks, if not days. This time, Flair didn't target The Giant at all, but instead turned his attention to the WCW U.S. title.

The Nature Boy won the U.S. belt from Konnan on July 7, 1996, at the Bash at the

Flair, who had once been "Rowdy" Roddy Piper's tag team partner, defeated Piper by disqualification at WCW's 1999 Great American Bash.

"Diamond" Dallas Page defeated Flair for the WCW World title on April 11, 1999, but Flair insisted he was still "the straw that stirs the drink" in WCW.

Beach pay-per-view event and defended the title successfully for four months before being forced to vacate the championship because of a shoulder injury.

Flair had to undergo surgery to repair the torn rotator cuff in his left shoulder, and was out of action until May 18, 1997, when he returned to the ring at Slamboree. At that card, he teamed with National Football League (NFL) star Kevin

Greene and "Rowdy" Roddy Piper to battle the NWO trio of Kevin Nash, Scott Hall, and Syxx.

From there, however, Flair's year took a sharp downward turn. He feuded violently with Piper. The Four Horsemen were in rare turmoil: they fired Jeff Jarrett, Arn Anderson retired, and Curt Hennig joined them only to quickly defect to the NWO. His stable of loyal wrestlers depleted, Flair disbanded the Horsemen on September 29, 1997.

The following year didn't seem to get any better for the Nature Boy. In April, WCW filed suit against Flair for breach of contract. The dispute centered around the fact that Flair had missed appearing at a WCW event in order to attend his son's amateur wrestling championship tournament. As a result, the Nature Boy wasn't even seen for much of the year.

However, when Flair did return, he did so in style. It happened on September 14, 1998, in Greenville, South Carolina, during a broadcast of *Monday Nitro*. Flair was there to tearfully thank the fans for their support over the years and to announce the reformation of the Four Horsemen, this time with a roster that included Dean Malenko, Steve McMichael, Chris Benoit, and Arn Anderson. The fans were jubilant, and Flair was energized.

A bit older, a bit smarter, and a bit more conniving, Flair decided to wage his battles not just in the ring, but in the corporate board room. On December 28, Flair battled WCW President (and NWO sympathizer) Eric Bischoff for administrative control of WCW. As the Horsemen shielded the ring, Flair thrashed Bischoff and forced him to submit to the figure-four leglock, then pinned him for good measure.

WCW, which had long been Flair's in spirit, was now officially his.

Three months later, the WCW World title was also Flair's, the result of a victory over his old rival Hulk Hogan at WCW's Uncensored pay-per-view on March 14, 1999. Not long after this long-awaited victory, though, Flair became drunk with power. He dictated who his challengers would be, and he directed his most threatening opponents into dangerous matches in an effort to keep them away from his championship.

Finally, on April 11, 1999, at WCW's Spring Stampede card, "Diamond" Dallas Page pinned the Nature Boy to capture the title in a four-way match that also included Hogan and Sting. It was a difficult loss for Flair. Eight days later, he was committed to an institution for psychiatric evaluation, because Roddy Piper and Ric's own son, David, himself a budding WCW star, felt that the Nature Boy was headed for a breakdown.

"The bottom line is Ric Flair, with a belt or without a belt, is the man in this business," Flair said just days after being released. "No matter what Piper, David, or Hogan say, Ric Flair is the straw that stirs the drink in WCW."

It seemed that way on June 13, 1999, when Flair defeated Piper by disqualification at the Great American Bash. But as the year drew to a close, the back injury Flair sustained in the 1975 plane crash came back to haunt him, and there were strong rumors that the Nature Boy would have to undergo another painful operation. David Flair, and not Ric Flair, was included in the bracketing of the late 1999 tournament to fill the WCW World title vacancy.

If Flair's career has been characterized by any one constant, though, it has been his ability to rise to any occasion, even when it seemed as if he'd been defeated once and for all. His never-say-die determination won him not just 16 world titles in the NWA, WCW, and the WWF, but global recognition as the single greatest professional wrestler of the 20th century.

Chronology

1949 Born Richard Morgan Fliehr in Edina, Minnesota, on February 25

1972 Makes his pro debut on December 10 and wrestles to a draw with "Scrap Iron" George Gadaski

1975 Suffers a career-threatening back injury in an airplane crash on October 4

1981 Wins his first NWA World title from Dusty Rhodes on September 17

1983 Wins his second NWA World title from Harley Race on November 24

1984 Wins his third NWA World title from Harley Race on March 23

Wins his fourth NWA World title from Kerry Von Erich on May 24

1986 Wins his fifth NWA World title from Dusty Rhodes on August 9

1987 Wins his sixth NWA World title from Ronnie Garvin on November 26

1989 Wins his seventh NWA World title from Rick Steamboat on May 7

1991 Wins his eighth NWA World title from Sting on January 11 (this championship is also acknowledged as Flair's first WCW World title)

Leaves WCW on July 1 and is stripped of the WCW World title

Makes his WWF debut, in Cornwall, Ontario, on September 10

1992 Wins his first WWF World title by winning the 30-man Royal Rumble on January 19

Wins his second WWF World title from Randy Savage on September 1

1993 Loses a "loser-leaves-federation" match to Curt Hennig on January 18

Returns to WCW, at SuperBrawl III in Asheville, North Carolina, on February 21

Wins his ninth NWA World title from Barry Windham on July 18

Wins his second WCW World title from Big Van Vader on December 27

1995 Wins his third WCW World title from Randy Savage on December 27

1996 Wins his fourth WCW World title from Randy Savage on February 11

1998 WCW files suit against Flair for breach of contract on April 21; still involved in a WCW lawsuit, Flair makes an emotional return to WCW on September 14; Flair wins administrative control of WCW from Eric Bischoff on December 28

1999 Wins his fifth WCW World title from Hulk Hogan on March 14

Further Reading

Burkett, Harry. "Ric Flair: The 10 Feats He Must Accomplish before He's Through." *The Wrestler* (June 1999): 58–61.

Hunter, Matt. *The Story of the Wrestler They Call "Hollywood" Hulk Hogan*. Philadelphia: Chelsea House Publishers, 2000.

Hunter, Matt. *Superstars of Men's Pro Wrestling*. Philadelphia: Chelsea House Publishers, 1998.

Norton, Blake. "Flair: 14 Titles and Counting." *WOW Magazine* (June 1999): 42–46.

"Q&A: Ric Flair" *Wrestler Digest* (Winter 1997): 94–100.

Rosenbaum, Dave. "The Dirt on the Dirtiest Player: Flair Couldn't Turn on the Women, So He Turned on Us!" *Wrestling Superstars* (August 1999): 42–46.

Rosenbaum, Dave. "Ric Flair's Hiatus: How Will It Affect His Game?" *Inside Wrestling Digest* (Spring 1999): 32–36.

Index

MATT HUNTER has spent nearly two decades writing about professional wrestling. In addition to this book on pro wrestling, the author's previously published volumes on the mat sport include *Jesse Ventura: The Story of the Wrestler They Call "The Body"*, *The Story of the Wrestler They Call "Hollywood" Hulk Hogan*, *Superstars of Pro Wrestling*, and *Wrestling Madness*. He has interviewed countless wrestlers on national television, photographed innumerable bouts from ringside, and written more magazine articles about the mat sport than he cares to calculate.